PORTRAIT OF A REVOLUTION

RUSSIA 1896-1924

Frédéric Rossif and Madeleine Chapsal

Translated by Hazel Kahn

Originally Published in France
as *Revolution d'Octobre*

LITTLE, BROWN AND COMPANY   Boston   Toronto

LIBRARY OF CONGRESS CATALOG CARD NO. 78–77453

FIRST ENGLISH LANGUAGE EDITION

Published in France under the title *Révolution d'Octobre.*
The photographs in this book are taken from Frédéric Rossif's film *Révolution d'Octobre.*

Lines from the poem "A Cloud in Trousers" are reprinted as they appear in *Mayakovsky* translated and edited by Herbert Marshall. Copyright © 1965 by Herbert Marshall. Reprinted by permission of the publishers, Hill and Wang, Inc. and Dobson Books Limited.

Lines from the poem "In All My Ways" by Boris Pasternak are reprinted from *In the Interlude: Poems 1945–1960* by Boris Pasternak, translated by Henry Kamen, with a Foreword by Sir Maurice Bowra and notes by George Katkov. English translation © Henry Kamen 1962. Reprinted by permission of A. D. Peters & Company.

Lines from Part 3 of the poem "Prayers for the First Forty Days of the Dead" by Sergei Alexandrovich Yesenin are reprinted as adapted by W. S. Merwin in *Selected Translations 1948–1968* by W. S. Merwin, published by Atheneum Publishers. Copyright © 1968 by W. S. Merwin.

Published simultaneously in Canada by Little, Brown & Company (Canada) Limited

PRINTED IN THE UNITED STATES OF AMERICA

"To the Emperor of all the Russias belongs supreme power. To obey his orders is the order of God Himself."

This was the basic law of Holy Russia.

3

The coronation of Czar Nicholas II of the Romanov family took place on May 14, 1896, in Moscow. He was the thirty-fifth Czar of all the Russias, following Simeon the Proud, Demetrius Donskoi, Ivan the Terrible, Boris Godunov, Peter the Great and Catherine the Great.

5

At the dedication of the statue of his father, Alexander III, Nicholas declared: "I intend to devote all my power to the happiness of our dear country, but at the same time I shall maintain the principle of autocracy just as firmly and unflinchingly as it was preserved by my unforgettable father."

Autocracy is a form of government in which the will of one person decides the destiny of all the people.

According to the system of *chins* (Table of Ranks) created by Peter the Great, every person who worked for the state, military and civilian alike, could be raised at any moment to the highest rank or put down to the lowest, according to the whim of the Czar. Prince or peasant, each one feared for the safety of the position he had achieved. And hoping for advancement, everyone redoubled his submission to the Czar.

In 1900 there were 100 million peasants in Russia, about eighty out of every one hundred persons. Their life expectancy was thirty years. Twelve Russian peasants had to subsist on what a single American worker consumed.

In 1861 Czar Alexander II, the Liberator, had freed the serfs, who were slaves, but he had not given them land of their own. The peasants did claim the land, however, and said: "Our backs belong to the Czar, but the land is ours."

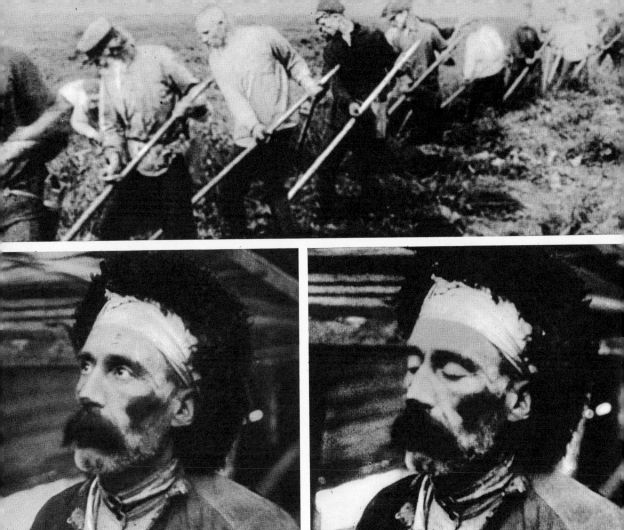

A new class began to emerge — the proletariat. There were two million workers. Unions were illegal and striking was an offense punishable by imprisonment. Workers worked thirteen hours a day. They earned fifteen rubles a month, the price of a pair of boots. Not until 1882 did it become illegal to employ in the mines children under twelve years old.

It was in the cities, under the watchful eye of the secret police — the Okhrana — that opposition to the system began. Anarchists, terrorists, Marxists, socialists, liberals — men, ideas, and theories came together, crisscrossed and opposed each other, and traveled all across Russia — as did the long convoys of political prisoners being deported to Siberia.

The writer Fedor Dostoevski called these places "the House of the Dead." From here those who were to be executed appealed to the Russian people: "Brothers and sisters, we address to you from our graves this last greeting which will be our testament. May our sad fate be the price of Russian freedom and may it bring to birth a better and more humane society! We salute our country. We salute all humanity."

Exiles met together and asked themselves: "What can we do? Where do we begin?"

Many believed the solution would be found through application of the ideas of Karl Marx, who advocated conquest of power by the working class (proletariat), so that all factories and production would be owned by the people.

Among those Russian exiles who were fascinated by those ideas was a young man, Vladimir Ilich Ulyanov. In 1895 he founded the League for Emancipation of the Working Class, which later became part of the Russian Social Democratic Labor Party. Vladimir's older brother Alexander had been hanged for having taken part in a plot to assassinate the Czar. Vladimir Ilich carried on in his place.

Arrested and condemned to three years of exile in Siberia, he wrote, he thought, and he prepared himself. He would return under the name of Lenin.

The high Orthodox clergy, previously the only spokesman of the people to the monarch, now became the auxiliary of the state police and unconditionally supported the autocracy.

On the night of February 8, 1904, the Japanese made a surprise attack on the Russian vessels at Port Arthur on the coast of southern Manchuria. The Czar declared war. A "small, happy war" against the Japanese was hoped for, but defeat was total. The Russian fleet at Tsushima was destroyed, Port Arthur fell, and the Russian troops at Mukden were crushed.

In addition to the disastrous war there were domestic uprisings. On Sunday, January 22, 1905, an unarmed crowd, led by a priest, Father Gapon, assembled at the Winter Palace in the capital city of St. Petersburg to present this plea to the sovereign: "We come to You, Sire, in search of truth and protection. Destroy the wall that is rising between You and Your people . . ." The soldiers of the guard fired without warning. Five hundred persons were killed and three thousand wounded. This carnage, known as "Bloody Sunday," severed the last bond which united the Czar to the Russian people.

In Moscow the Semionovski guard regiment wiped out a workers' revolt with gunfire. The sailors of the battleship *Potemkin* at Odessa mutinied and killed their officers. Trepov, governor general of St. Petersburg, ordered the soldiers charged with suppressing the rebellion: "Above all, don't spare the bullets."

17

"Seven condemned to death — two in St. Petersburg, one in Moscow, two in Penza, two in Riga; four executions — two in Kharkov, one in Vilna, one in Odessa." Every day in every newspaper this news was repeated.

"You say you are committing all these horrors in order to restore peace and order. You say this is the only way to pacify the people and put down the revolution. But that is false. You will not be able to pacify the people without satisfying their most elementary demands: for justice and for land."

With these words, Leo Tolstoi, the greatest Russian writer, challenged the Czar.

19

When Tolstoi was buried in 1910, the peasants carried a banner which read: "Leo Nikolaevich, the memory of the good which you have done will never die for us; the peasants of Yasnaya Polyana henceforth are orphans."

Czar Nicholas II did not listen to Leo Tolstoi or to the people. His decisions were dictated by his wife, Alexandra Feodorovna of the Hesse-Darmstadt family of Germany and granddaughter of Queen Victoria of Great Britain. The Czarina herself was dominated by Grigori Efimovich Rasputin. Rasputin was a mystic, a debauchee, an illiterate and a seer. He was called "a man of God." People believed he could predict the future, ward off dangers and cure sicknesses.

The heir apparent, the Czar's son Alexis, was afflicted with hemophilia, a hereditary disease of the Hesse-Darmstadt family. Rasputin convinced the Czarina that only he could keep her son alive. The presence of Rasputin as a favorite in the court completed the discredit of the sovereigns in the eyes of the people.

For ten years political blunders alternated with halfway measures. After the Revolution of 1905, the workers of St. Petersburg organized the first Soviet, or Workers' Council, of St. Petersburg. Then the Czar agreed to the formation of a parliament, the Duma. The first Duma was dissolved after seventy-four days. The second Duma lasted one hundred and three days. A new electoral law limited popular representation, and the third Duma was almost exclusively composed of members of the nobility. The fourth Duma, elected in 1912, met only four times and was adjourned without fixing a date for future meeting.

Unrest grew throughout the country. The Social Democratic Labor Party was torn by dissension. The followers of Lenin, called Bolsheviks, felt that power could be gained only through a revolution. The minority group of the party, the Mensheviks, believed that parliamentary methods could accomplish the same goal over a period of time.

During this period more than two hundred political assassinations took place, including those of Prefect von Launitz, Prime Minister Stolypin and Grand Duke Sergius, the Czar's uncle.

But Russian absolutism would never yield to the opposition except under the blow of military defeat.

On June 28, 1914, Archduke Franz Ferdinand of Austria and the Archduchess were assassinated by a Serbian nationalist at Sarajevo, which was then part of Austria-Hungary. On July 28, 1914, the emperor of Austria-Hungary, Franz Josef, declared war on Serbia. The southern Slavs appealed for Russian protection. On July 31, 1914, Czar Nicholas II ordered general mobilization. On the first of August, Germany declared war on Russia.

At first, victory was easy. Russian troops advanced on all fronts. Russian generals Samsonov and Rennenkampf penetrated German lines and entered East Prussia. German generals Hindenburg and Ludendorff arrived at the front and prepared the counteroffensive. It was the battle of Tannenberg, the first great Russian defeat.

General Sukhomlinov, the Russian Minister of War, declared: "I am confident because of the vastness of our territory. I am counting on the mud to make our roads impassable, and to win the war I am relying on the good graces of St. Nicholas, patron saint of Holy Russia."

The soldiers listened instead to the propaganda that condemned the imperialist war and appealed to brotherhood: "Your brothers are speaking. The war is over. It is the Czar's war. We are workers and peasants like you. We do not want to fight against you. You are killing your brothers."

By the end of 1916, two and a half million Russian soldiers had died, four and a half million had been wounded and one million had deserted. The soldiers had abandoned the war to work for the Revolution.

More than ten million of the twelve million men in the army were peasants. They had wanted land for centuries. The Czar, the Duma, the revolutionary socialists, the representatives of the peasants — everyone had promised them land after victory.

"What good will land be if I no longer exist? I will no longer need it." The peasants left on foot for their villages: The Russian earth — nothing dammed its flow, nothing limited it. Indolently it let men and ideas enter, only to close again behind them.

Four hundred thousand men were industrial
workers in Petrograd, the new name for St.
Petersburg. They were the most highly organized proletariat in all Russia. Exasperated by
military reverses, the prolongation of the war,
and the famine, they had only one means of
protest: to strike. Throughout the winter walkout followed walkout and demonstrations were
continuous. Their slogans were: "Down with
the famine-Czar! Down with the war!"

February 23, 1917, was International Women's Day. The textile workers went on strike and organized a demonstration. The police did nothing to stop them. The metal workers joined the strike on February 24. By February 25 it had become a general strike. On February 26 some of the troops in Petrograd joined the strikers. Workers and soldiers were beginning to take over the city.

The Czar cabled from the front: "I order that the disorders in the capital be stopped by tomorrow. They cannot be tolerated in this grave time of war with Germany and Austria."

On February 27, the Volinsk Regiment, of which the Czar was colonel,
went over to the insurrection. It drew
in its wake other regiments which had
traditionally been the most faithful
defenders of the empire.

General Brusilov, hero of the war against Austria-Hungary, declared, "Between the Czar and Russia, I choose Russia." The police alone continued to defend the power of the Czar. The insurgents stormed the arsenal, the courthouse, the Ministry of the Interior, and the Fortress of Peter and Paul. General Khabalov cabled the Czar: "Order cannot be restored in Petrograd."

"By the grace of God, we, Nicholas II, Emperor of all Russia, King of Poland and Grand Duke of Finland, let it be known to all our faithful subjects that we have thought it good to abdicate from the throne of the Russian state, and to lay down the supreme power. May God help Russia. Nicholas II."

44

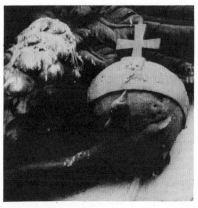

The Czar had fallen. The last of the Romanovs, the last of the descendants of one of the oldest and most powerful monarchies, had stepped down after five days of rioting. A series of halfway measures and partial reforms, concessions made in fear and withdrawn once the storm had passed, had worn away the power of the Czar and had strengthened the Revolution.

In his message *Greetings to the February Revolution,* Maxim Gorki, the writer, reflected: "The Russian people have espoused liberty. We hope that this union will give birth to new men, strong men, in our physically and spiritually exhausted country. But we must not forget that we are all people of the past."

Autocracy, secrecy, and Czarist power no longer existed. The Soviet of Workers' and Soldiers' Deputies controlled the streets. The bourgeois members of parliament prepared a provisional government. They arrested the Okhrana agents, the Czar's secret police. They freed in joy the political prisoners; singing, they buried the victims of the Revolution.

The Provisional Government was composed of
a majority of bourgeois deputies of parliament.
Prince Lvov, a liberal member of the nobility,
presided over the Provisional Government, and
the intellectual Milyukov dominated it.

The Petrograd Soviet immediately took note of the existence of dual powers by its Order Number One concerning the army: "All military units are under the command of the Soviet of Workers' and Soldiers' Deputies and its committees."

The exiles returned from all parts of the world. The most famous and the most eagerly awaited, Vladimir Ilich Lenin, arrived on the third of April, and immediately put everything once more in question.

In his April Theses he proclaimed that the Workers' and Peasants' Soviet should grant no support whatsoever to the Provisional Government because of its capitalistic nature; that land should be placed under the control of local soviets of farm workers and peasants, and that all banks should merge into one national bank. He demanded the abolition of the police, the army and the civil service, and the establishment of a people's army to replace the regular army. He suggested that the name of the Social Democratic Party be changed to the Bolshevik Communist Party and that the party prepare to seize power.

The one obstacle to Lenin and the Bolsheviks was Alexander Kerenski, a lawyer and a member of the Social Revolutionary Party. Kerenski, who had been Minister of Justice and then Minister of War, quickly replaced Prince Lvov as head of the Provisional Government. Kerenski sympathized with the proletariat and the peasants. However, he was a moderate and did not believe in violent overthrow of the government. He did believe that Russia should continue to fight against Germany. His views were not popular with the Bolsheviks.

The government was powerless. It could not satisfy the increasing demands of the workers for higher wages. It could not nationalize the land, which would please the peasants, nor prevent the encroachments of peasants, which would please the great landowners. It could make neither war nor peace. In contrast to the ineffectiveness of the Provisional Government, the slogans of the Bolsheviks gained ground: an end to the senseless war; an end to speculation and treason; all power to the all-Russian Soviet of workers', soldiers' and peasants' delegates; and bread, peace and freedom.

The only policy of the Provisional Government
was to continue the war. Kerenski launched a
general offensive. He declared: "You will carry
peace, law, truth and justice at the end of your
bayonets." The supporters of the war went into
the streets: "War until total victory. Russia is a
great power and it is our duty to defend her."
On July 3, 1917, a popular insurrection against
the war threatened the Provisional Government.
Kerenski ordered his troops to fire into the
crowd.

Although Petrograd was in turmoil, the rest of the immense Russian territory was quiet. Tired of waiting for the promised reforms, peasant soldiers back from the trenches took matters into their own hands. They expropriated property and threatened to burn down the homes of the nobles. Cossacks were sent on punitive missions by the same Provisional Government which had a majority of Revolutionary Socialists representing the peasantry.

Kerenski wanted to crush the revolt. On July 6 an order for the arrest of the most important Bolshevik leaders was issued. Trotsky, Kamenev and Lunacharsky were imprisoned in the Fortress of Peter and Paul. Zinoviev and Lenin had time to escape.

Lenin, disguised and carrying false identification papers, took refuge in Finland. Far from Petrograd, he sent many messages to the Soviet and edited a manual of revolutionary action.

Kerenski believed he had rid himself of the opposition and he promised a strong government. But his great military offensive failed. The southern front fell apart. In the Ukraine, Finland, Poland and White Russia, the separatist and national movements grew stronger. Kerenski's only support came from the army.

Kornilov was named commander in chief. His bravery was legendary. In the eyes of the bourgeoisie and the army he became the savior of the country.

Kornilov, strengthened by his popularity, decided to seize power from the Provisional Government. He ordered the Cossack division known as the Savage Division to march on Petrograd and he delivered an ultimatum: "I, General Kornilov, declare that the government is betraying the country. All of you who feel a Russian heart beating in your breast and all of you who believe in God, pray to the Lord for the salvation of our native land. I, General Kornilov, the son of a Cossack peasant, swear that after the victory I will lead the people to democracy."

Both Lenin's Bolsheviks and Kerenski's Provisional Government opposed Kornilov.

65

Resistance was organized in the streets of Petrograd. The Committee for the Defense of the Revolution was formed at the call of the Soviet. The Bolshevik Red Guards were mobilized and the workers' militias, dissolved in July, took up arms again and organized the defense of the city. Kerenski removed Kornilov. The railway workers stopped military convoys headed for the capital. The coup of Kornilov was vanquished without a shot having been fired.

The real victors were the Bolsheviks. The Revolution had finally found leaders who knew what they wanted, who stated their objectives and realized them. Now the struggle mounted between the Bolsheviks and Kerenski's Provisional Government.

On September 25, Kerenski shuffled his cabinet for the last time. On the same day Trotsky was elected president of the Petrograd Soviet. Immediately throughout the whole country the same slogan was launched, repeated, and expounded: "All power to the soviets!"

Lenin wrote from his refuge: "The Bolsheviks, a majority in the soviets, can and must take power into their own hands. We must formulate our program in the clearest and most effective manner: peace for the people, land for the peasants, and confiscation of outrageous profits. Remember the words of Karl Marx; ponder them: 'Insurrection must be considered an art.'"

In factory after factory and barracks after barracks, the Bolshevik orators removed the last doubts and hesitations. Trotsky was everywhere at once.

On October 9, the Petrograd Soviet decided to form a Military Revolutionary Committee. The next day, Lenin secretly assembled the members of the Central Committee of the Bolshevik party. Those present were Lenin, Sverdlov, Zinoviev, Kamenev, Trotsky, Stalin, Uritsky, Dzerzhinsky, Alexandra Kollontai, Bubnov, Sokolnikov and Lomov-Oppokov.

The following resolution was adopted: "Realizing that armed insurrection is inevitable, and that the time for it has fully matured, the Central Committee enjoins all party organizations to be guided accordingly, and to discuss and decide all practical questions . . . from this point of view."

On October 13, the Baltic fleet put itself under the authority of the Military Revolutionary Committee. On October 18, a meeting of the committee of the Petrograd regiments decided: "The Petrograd garrison no longer recognizes the Provisional Government. The Petrograd Soviet is our government." The Military Revolutionary Committee was to plan the insurrection: every detachment of Red Guards and every detachment of troops was assigned a precise mission.

Workers of the Vyborg sector would control the bridges and occupy the Finland Station of Petrograd.

Red Guards of the Petrograd sector would keep under surveillance and if necessary blockade the Cossacks and the Paul and Vladimir Military Schools.

Soldiers of the Finland Regiment would occupy the Dvortsovy and Nikolaevski bridges and would control the quays of the Grand Neva.

There remained the Fortress of Peter and Paul. Whoever controlled Peter and Paul controlled Petrograd. The soldiers of that fortress were not to be relied upon. The Military Revolutionary Committee prepared to attack the fortress. Then Trotsky went to the fortress alone and spoke to the soldiers. He won them over with his words. Peter and Paul passed into the hands of the Soviets.

The cruiser *Aurora,* which had an entirely pro-Bolshevik crew, dropped anchor in the Neva and leveled its cannon on the Winter Palace, seat of Kerenski's Provisional Government.

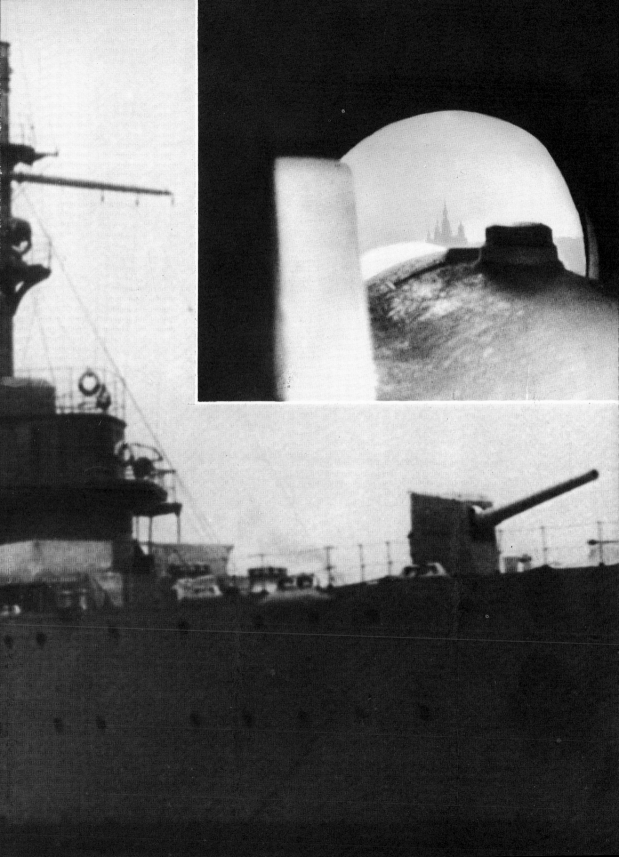

On October 24, Kerenski and the Provisional Government, having taken refuge in the Winter Palace, former residence of the czars, were virtually surrounded and cut off from the rest of Petrograd.

Kerenski cabled General Cheremisov: "I order the dispatch by rail to Petrograd of all Cossack regiments with all their artillery."

As matters stood that day, for the defense of the Winter Palace the Provisional Government was able to count on a battalion of two hundred women, personally organized by Kerenski.

In the course of the day a thousand cadets from the military schools of Petrograd joined the women's battalion. Kerenski called together all his ministers in special session and declared that he was prepared to defend the liberty of the new Russian state, even at the cost of his life. Thereupon he had his car secretly readied and left the Winter Palace to meet the expected reinforcements.

By noon on October 25, the State Bank, the Electric Works, the Post Office building, and the telegraph agency were in the hands of the insurgents. The Provisional Government continued to meet. Dr. Kishkin, Minister of Social Planning, was put in charge of the defense of the Winter Palace. With the chiefs of the different detachments he took stock of the forces at his disposal. There were two hundred Cossacks, one thousand student officers from military schools, and two hundred women soldiers. At five o'clock in the afternoon, the Provisional Government issued the following message to the Russian people: "Citizens, irresponsible lunatics have provoked a revolt against the only government chosen by the people — the Provisional Government. Citizens, you must help the Provisional Government fight against the enemies of liberty whose purpose is to destroy the gains won by the Revolution and the future of our beloved country. Citizens, rally around the Provisional Government to defend its authority in the name of order and the welfare of all."

The encirclement of the Winter Palace continued. Soon it would be complete. Lenin declared: "We must, at any price, arrest the Provisional Government this evening, after disarming the military students and crushing them if they resist. The Provisional Government is faltering; we must finish it off at all costs."

At six o'clock in the evening, the Military Revolutionary Committee issued an ultimatum to the Palace: "You have twenty minutes to surrender."

The ministers of the Provisional Government decided not to reply to the ultimatum. The insurgents attacked.

The women's battalion and the military students withdrew inside the Winter Palace.

The Red Guards took the entrance to the Winter Palace.

At ten o'clock the Red Guards took the north wing of the Winter Palace.

At two o'clock in the morning, the women's battalion and the remaining students surrendered.

Ten minutes later, Antonov-Ovseenko, secretary of the Military Revolutionary Committee, entered the Room of the Marshals: "In the name of the Military Revolutionary Committee, I declare you, ministers of the Provisional Government, under arrest."

On October 26, 1917, Petrograd buried its dead
— the young cadets according to ancient rites,
the Red Guards to the chanting of revolutionary
hymns.

The slogan "All power to the soviets" became a reality. The new government called itself the Council of People's Commissars. All its members were Bolsheviks. Lenin was chairman. Trotsky was in charge of Foreign Affairs. Rykov was in charge of Interior. Stalin was entrusted with the position of Commissar of Nationalities. Lunacharsky was the People's Commissar for Education. At two o'clock in the morning of October 27, 1917, the Council of People's Commissars proclaimed:

"All private land ownership is to be abolished in Russia forever. All land within the borders of the country is to become the property of all the people. The land will be for the use of the people who cultivate it. All citizens of the state have the right to use the land, on the condition that it be cultivated by their own families."

But there was also the war. German troops controlled a part of Russian territory. Lenin declared: "The workers' and peasants' government created by the October Revolution proposes to all peoples at war and to their governments that talks concerning a democratic peace, without annexations or reparations, begin immediately. The Russian workers and peasants are certain that the proletariat of the West will help them to carry through the task of re-establishing peace." Peace negotiations between the Soviet Republic and imperial Germany began on December 9, 1917, in Brest-Litovsk. The Bolsheviks were divided as to policy.

Trotsky, the delegate to Brest-Litovsk, decided that neither war nor peace was the answer. The Germans resumed the offensive and penetrated the front. Now peace had to be accepted at any price.

On March 3, 1918, Germany dictated the terms of peace. Germany annexed Poland and Lithuania and the part of western Russia bordering them called White Russia. The Soviets were forced to recognize the independence of the Ukraine and Finland.

Russia had lost one-fourth of her population. The Mensheviks, the Revolutionary Socialists, and the patriots were unanimous in their criticism: "A shameful, unprecedented and dishonorable peace."

Lenin replied: "Every revolutionary will absolve us and recognize that a shameful peace was necessary. If I accept peace when the army is in flight and can do nothing but flee, I accept it so that nothing worse happens. Nothing is more important now than our revolution. We must keep it out of danger at all costs."

On March 12, the Soviet Government established itself in Moscow, which once again became the capital of Russia. Lenin issued new slogans from the Kremlin. He said: "We, the Bolsheviks, have convinced Russia and we have conquered her. Now we must govern her."

To the propagandists who were about to travel throughout the country, he was specific: "The enemy is disorganization. It is you, comrades, who must take up the fight against this curse. A difficult but fruitful task awaits you. You must organize the rural economy and consolidate Soviet power. You will have helpers because we know that every worker and every peasant who lives by the work of his hands knows in his heart that nothing but Soviet power can save him from famine and annihilation. And we can save Russia."

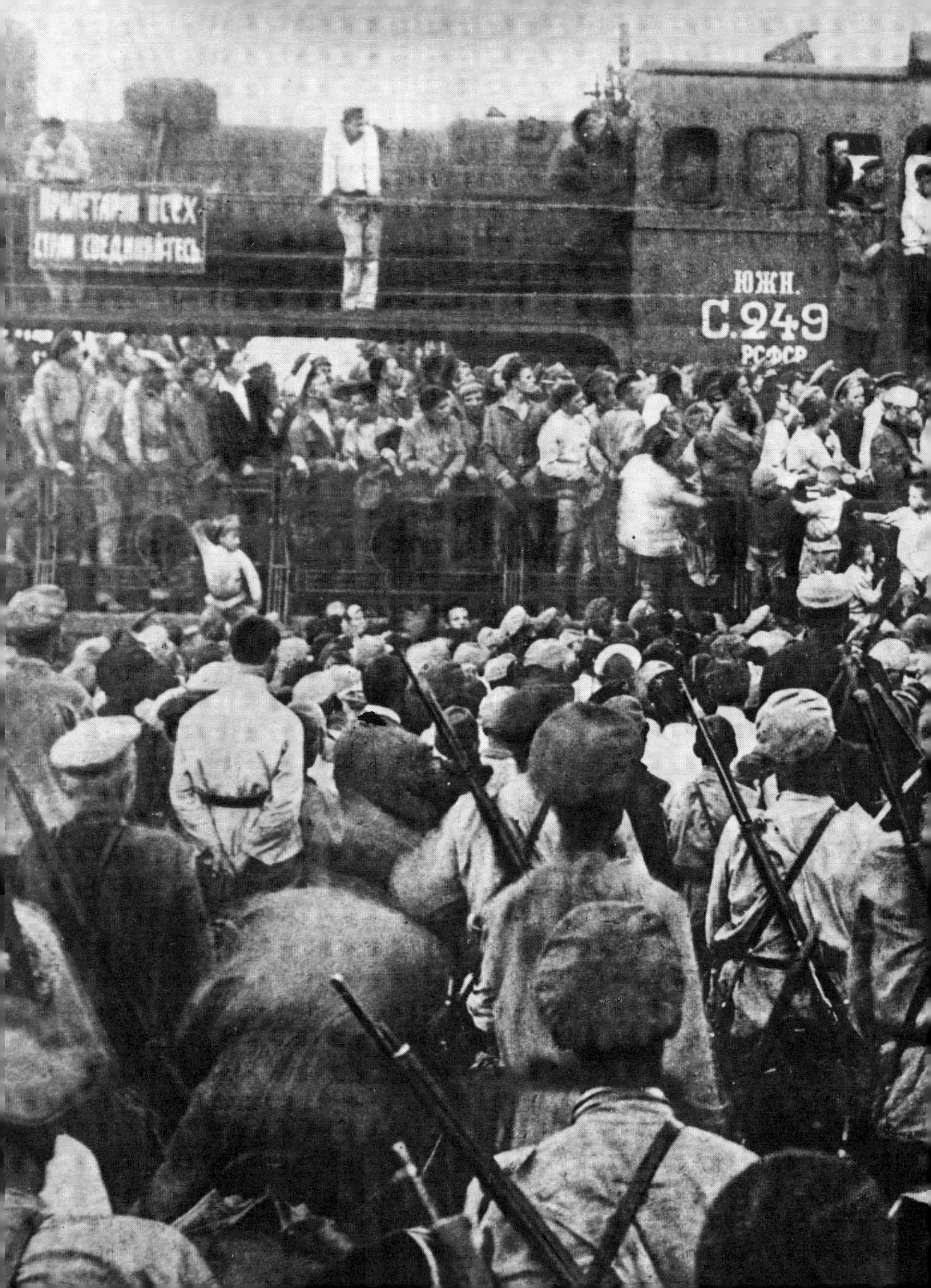
ПРОЛЕТАРИИ ВСЕХ
СТРАН СОЕДИНЯЙТЕСЬ
ЮЖН.
С.249
РСФСР

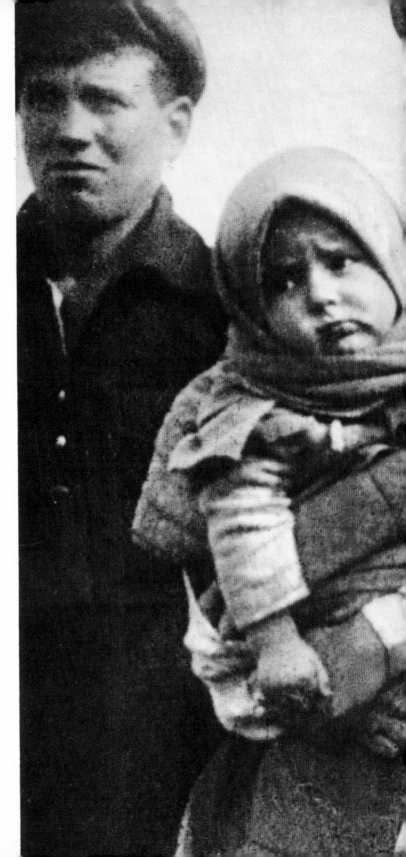

Maxim Gorki wrote: "The boundless plain has the dangerous power of emptying man, of draining his desires. The peasant goes beyond the borders of his village. He looks at the void surrounding him and, sometime later, feels that this void has flowed into his own soul. Nowhere around him can he perceive lasting traces of his labor or creation."

And so he searches for God.

The Russian Orthodox Church, which included the majority of the Slavic peasants, openly opposed Soviet power.

The Russian Orthodox Church, the former Czarist officers humiliated by the October Revolution, the bourgeoisie and the landowners terrified by the idea of nationalization, some generals, and a group of Revolutionary Socialists formed the disparate group that came to be known as the White Army.

But there was now a central government of the Soviet Republic. Its armed enemies, the White Army, were no longer simply the opposition. They were rebels.

The most important leader of the rebel White Army, Baron Admiral Kolchak, was proclaimed, "the supreme regent of Russia."

The White armies immediately committed acts which set the majority of the population against them: seizure of land by the former owners and summary executions of peasants accused of Bolshevism.

On the White Army propaganda posters everything appeared simple: Cossacks, and Czech,
English, French and American armies were all
united against the Soviet monster.

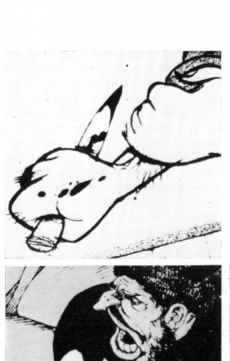
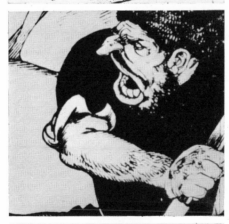

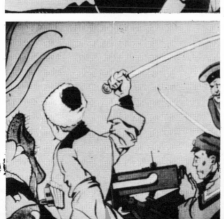

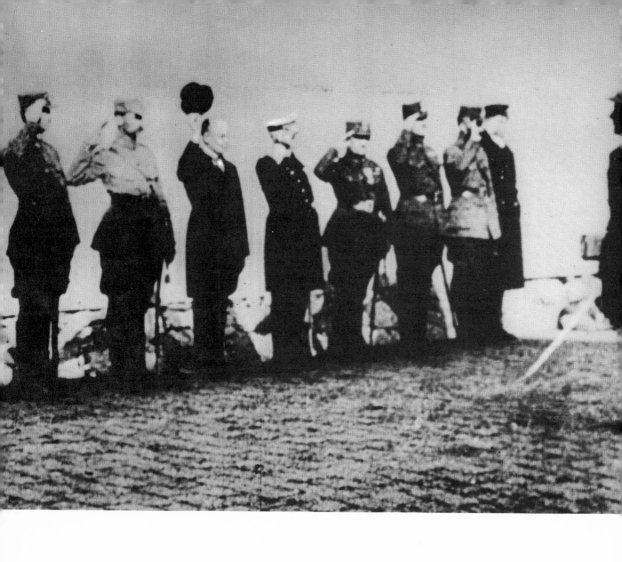

In reality, the intervening foreign powers lacked sufficient resources, were vague and hesitant in deciding their objectives, and in addition found themselves dispersed over a five-thousand-mile front.

The English kept watch on the French and the French kept watch on the English. The Japanese kept watch on the Americans and the Americans kept watch on the Japanese.

It was a politically and tactically divided White Army that converged on Moscow from the Ukraine, Siberia, northern Russia and the Black Sea.

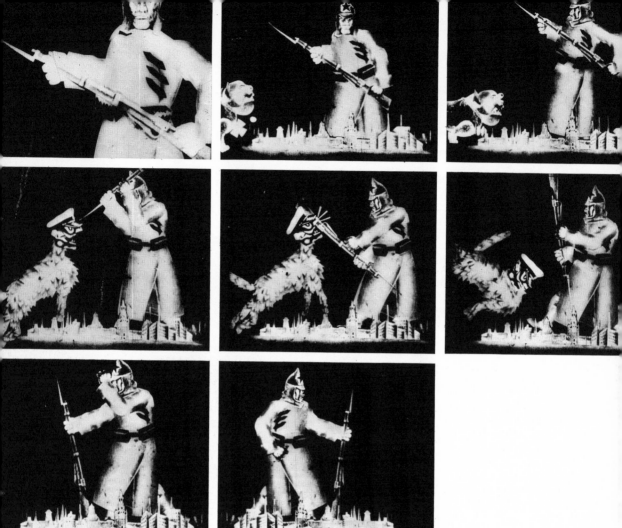

On the Red Army propaganda posters everything also appeared simple. But in truth the members of the Red Army were peasants without military knowledge and without a military tradition, forced to confront professional armies.

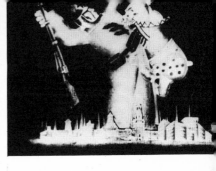

These men, without uniforms, took an oath to the Red Army: "I, son of the working people and citizen of the Soviet Republic, take the title of soldier of the peasants' and workers' army. I pledge that I will strictly observe revolutionary discipline. I pledge that for the cause of socialism I will spare neither my energy nor my life. If I fail to keep this promise, may I be punished by the inflexible arm of revolutionary law."

The Red Army found its source of inspiration in Leon Trotsky.

The legendary hero of the Red cavalry, Vasili Ivanovich Chapaev, became the symbol of the people's soldier. Endowed with limitless courage, almost illiterate, he was a general at the age of thirty-four and died while trying, though wounded, to swim across the Ural River.

The young and fiery Mikhail Tukhachevski, second lieutenant in the Imperial Guard, chose to serve the Soviet power. He became a general at the age of twenty-five. A brilliant tactician of field warfare, he was nicknamed the Red Napoleon.

The Czar and his family were being held at Ekaterinburg. The White armies were approaching and the Ekaterinburg Soviet suddenly decided to execute the imperial family. They were shot during the night of July 16, 1918.

On October 20, 1919, the troops of the White General Yudenich were at the gates of Petrograd. Petrograd, cradle of the Revolution, prepared its barricades. Tsarskoye Selo, the czars' summer palace, fifteen miles from the city, had fallen to the White Army.

The Bolsheviks mobilized the Red Guard and sent their last men to the front. Gorki said of them: "These are the Russians who are going to battle for the triumph of justice. Only yesterday the world considered them almost savages and today, nearly dead from hunger, they are as fervent and brave as veterans."

Yudenich ordered his troops to take the hill of Pulkovo, the last natural defense of Petrograd.

The regular troops, the Red Guards and the workers' detachments defended Petrograd with heroic fervor.

The attack of the White Army was thwarted and the Red Army was on the counteroffensive, pushing the troops of Yudenich beyond the Estonian border. Contrary to all expectations the soldiers of the people's army defeated the professional soldiers.

Lenin said to them: "Red soldiers, know that you are leading a bloody and desperate fight. Contempt of death must fill you and assure victory. Attack and not defense must be your motto."

Felix Dzerzhinsky, who fought for the revolutionary movement for twenty-five years and had spent ten years of his life in the Czar's prisons, was appointed by Lenin to head a special commission called the Cheka to combat speculation, sabotage and counterrevolution.

The Cheka was one of the instruments of wartime communism. Its purpose was to fight against the Revolutionary Socialists who were making attempts on Lenin's life and to bring an end to the looting, corruption among civil servants, officers' conspiracies, sabotage, and the growing anarchy throughout the country.

Lenin said: "Can one be human in the midst of such savage conflict? We know what we want, no one else can do it for us. Morality outside human society does not exist for us. For us morality is totally subordinate to the interests of the proletarian struggle."

The people in the cities lacked supplies. There was no more soap; there were no more shoes; there was no more clothing. The daily bread ration amounted to less than two ounces. People lined up for everything, and for hours at a time.

Troops were sent to compel the peasants to deliver their wheat. In many villages these soldiers met with armed resistance. When requisitions were announced, the peasants mobilized and went to the aid of the threatened villages.

Even pigsties were considered good hiding places. The requisitioned wheat did not always reach its destination. Trains were attacked and looted. It took as many as three hundred men to guard a train loaded with wheat.

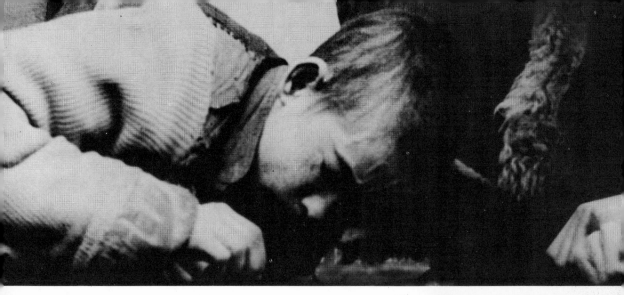

Lenin declared: "We are now faced with the most fundamental task of all human society: to combat famine."

Russia suffered the worst famine of her history. Nearly thirty-six million people were victims. Cannibalism began to appear.

Antonov-Ovseenko declared: "Bodies are used as food. The families of those who have died of hunger must guard the tombs during the first few days after burial."

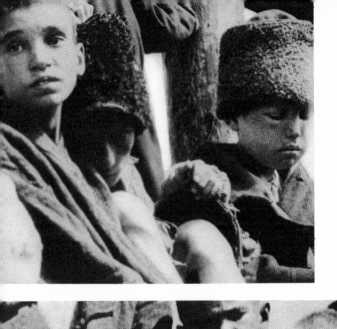
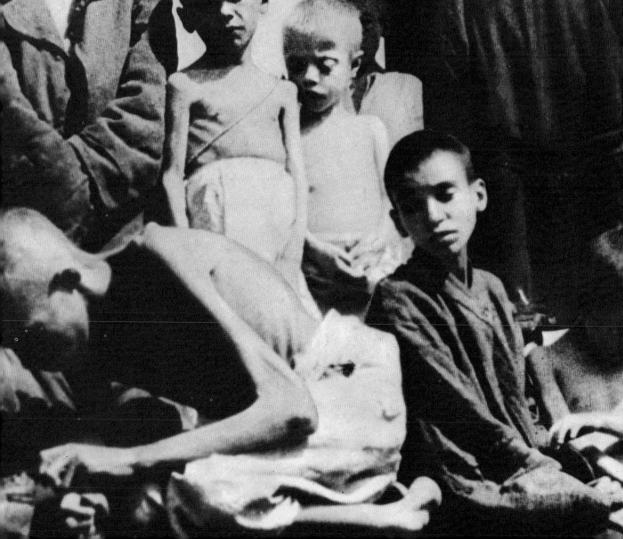

Hunger and epidemics forced millions of persons to the roads of Russia — the workers going from the cities toward the countryside and the peasants from the countryside toward the cities. All went with one purpose: to find food.

Lenin declared: "When the people are starving and unemployment is widespread, the person who hides extra wheat, the person who deprives the state of even one pound of fuel, is the worst of all criminals."

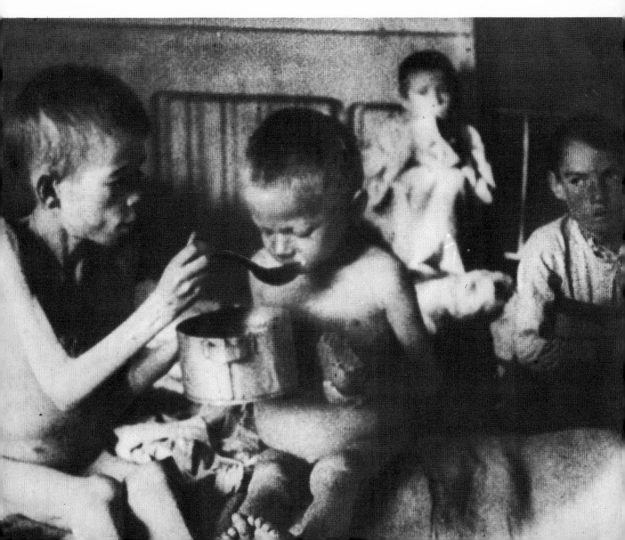

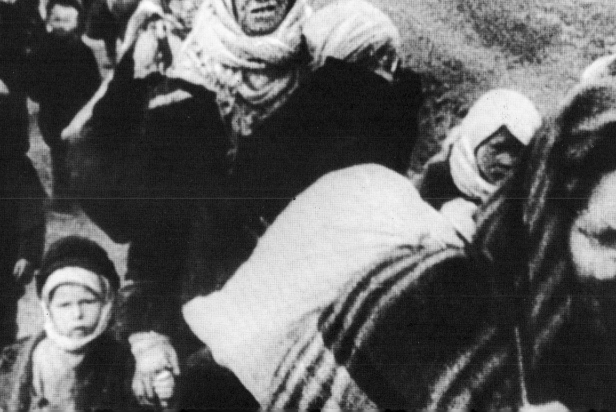

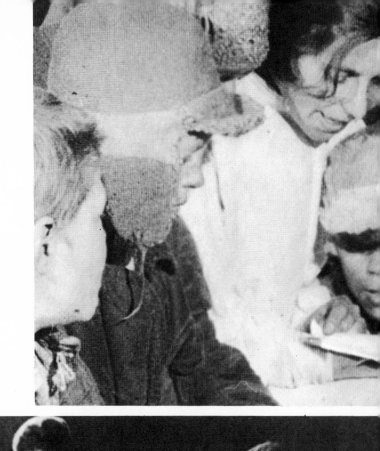

Millions of children, orphaned by the war, epidemics and famine, grouped together in bands and traveled throughout Russia. They attacked, looted and killed. They had to be brought together, lodged and fed. They had to be taught how to live.

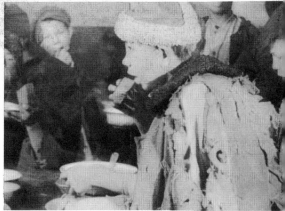

The civil war was over by the end of 1920. The toll was heavy: eight million dead, a destroyed country, empty villages and a ruined agriculture. For the Soviet power the most difficult tasks of all now remained: to gain peace and organize their life.

Lenin launched a new watchword: "Communism is Soviet power plus electricity. Without this we will remain a country of small peasants. Only when the entire country has electricity, when industry, agriculture and transportation are based on modern techniques, only then will we have won for good."

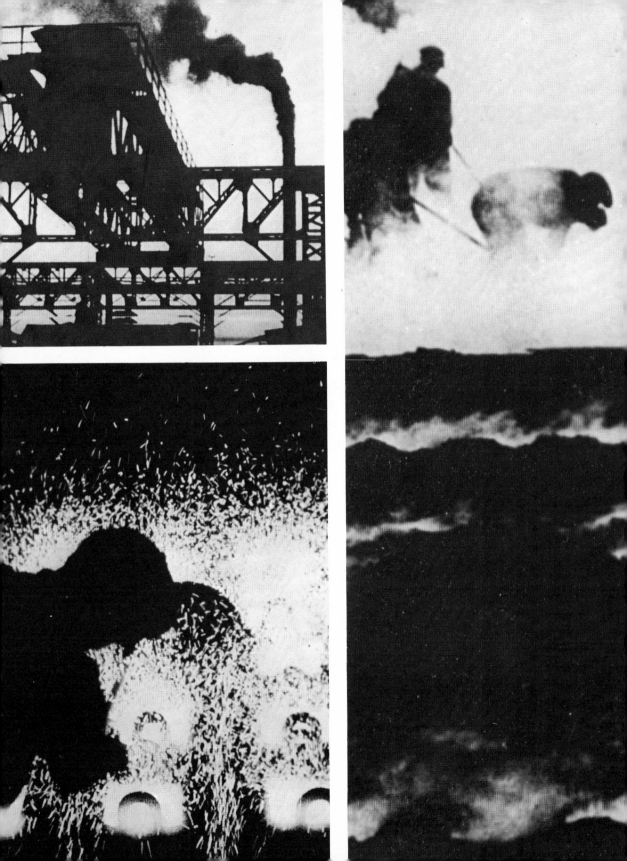

The sailors of the fortress of Kronstadt, the "ornament and glory" of the Russian Revolution, did not adjust well to peace. On February 28, 1921, they revolted with cries of "Death to the Bolsheviks!" On March 16, the Petrograd garrison and sixty thousand men from the Cheka, under the command of General Tukhachevski, crushed the revolt. The next day Tukhachevski was able to announce: "There is no longer any sign of life at Kronstadt."

Faced with the wave of discontent, extreme poverty, strikes, and in the midst of the Kronstadt revolt, Lenin decided that it was time to end the wartime communism and adopt a new economic policy.

By March 29, 1921, the peasants could sell their products freely after paying a state tax. By May 17, craftsmen were allowed to trade openly. By July 7, factories having fewer than twenty workers were denationalized.

The results of the NEP, the New Economic Policy, were immediate. Work resumed and production increased. The city dweller was better fed and the peasant lived better.

The Revolution thrust into view a throng of people who wanted not only liberty but knowledge and education as well. Lunacharsky, Commissar of Public Education, told the poets: "And now, everything is possible."

Sergei Esenin, the beloved poet, fervently sympathized with the Soviets. He was the poet of the Russian countryside. Esenin described himself in this way:

> He was the son of a peasant.
> His story is very short.
> He had black hair,
> And gentle blue eyes.

> I have now decided and will not turn back:
> I am abandoning the fields of my fathers.
> The land of birch trees and clear skies
> will never again see me walking barefoot.
> Back there, at my parents' house,
> a young girl in white waits for me.
> I can no longer protect my youth.

To a young horse who was trying to catch up with a train Esenin said:

> the darling
> the little idiot
> where does he think he's running
> Doesn't he know that all his kind
> have lost to the steel cavalry

And he said:

> Listening to a song in the silence,
> My beloved, with another beloved,
> Will perhaps think of me
> As one thinks of a solitary flower.

Lenin proclaimed: "Of all the arts, the cinema is the most important for us."

Dziga Vertov founded a film group in 1920. He was the editor, producer and director of the first Soviet news films. He invented the theory of *Kino-Pravda,* or *cinéma-vérité:* bourgeois settings must be abolished; life must be captured unawares; filming must be done from within crowds.

Boris Pasternak.

Vladimir Mayakovski.

Pasternak, the most private of the revolutionary poets, said:

> Always and still grasping the thread
> Of fate and acts, thereby
> To live, to think, to feel, to love
> And blaze discovery.

Vladimir Mayakovski, gigantic, herculean and thundering, was the mos courageous of the verbal fighters.

> Here we are standing,
> torn from the stomach of the earth
> by the cesarean of war.
> We celebrate you,
> Day of riots,
> revolts
> and revolutions.
> You who move,
> fracturing skulls,
> day of our resurrection,
> I exult,
> the world is finally adult.

Our old tailor
was no longer working
according to our size.
Well, what difference!
` might be ridiculous,
's garment,
   it is ours.
:e room for us!
 'y
 ` the dust of the theaters
   otto will burn proudly:
   al.
   'by, stop,
   d admire.

   ' true Communist
   an who knew how to burn all the bridges.
   ' of jogging along, Communists.
   ' future, a leap!

   le ones
   . lay your love on a violin.
   ' crude lay their love on a drum.
   t you can't, like me, turn inside out entirely,
   d nothing but human lips become!

   /ou like —
   be furious flesh elemental,
   — changing to tones that the sunset arouses —
   ou like —
   be extraordinarily gentle,
   (a man but — a cloud in trousers!

   ..verything is made
   or the pleasure
   of the big children that we are.
   We are going to invent
   new roses.

In his last public speech Lenin said: "Our party, a handful of men in comparison with the masses, must remake everything and it will remake everything. We have already proven that this is not Utopia, but is a task that can fill entire lifetimes. We have already realized this and it has been done. But everything must be re-shaped so that the majority of workers and peasants can say to us: 'You have obtained such results that no reasonable man would any longer wish to return to the past.' This has not yet been accomplished. Much remains to be done. When our adversaries say to us: 'Look, Lenin himself admits that the Bolsheviks made mistakes,' I answer them: 'Yes, it is true, but you know that our mistakes are of a different nature from yours.' The main problem for us, the Communists, must be the choice of the right men and the practical testing of the results of their work."

On January 21, 1924,
the news shook Russia:
Lenin was dead.

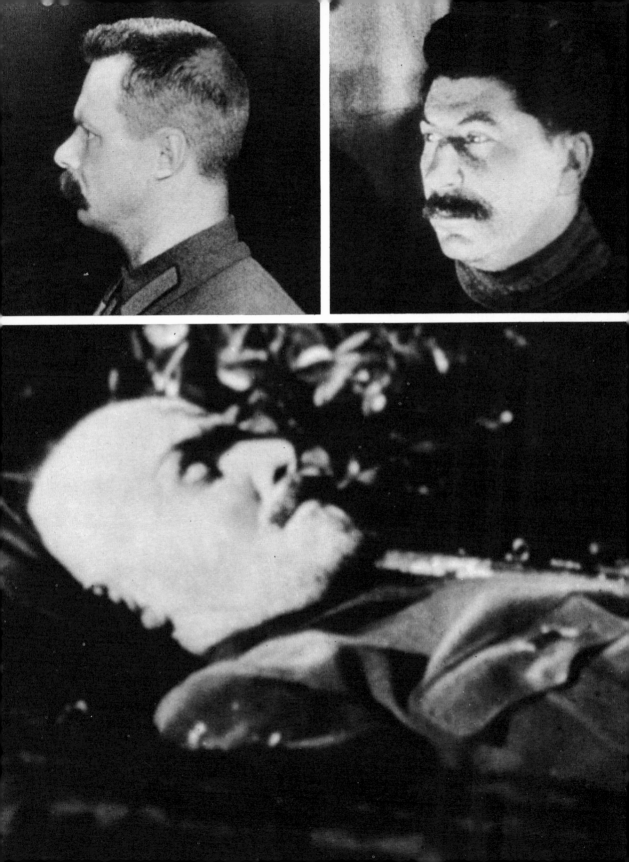

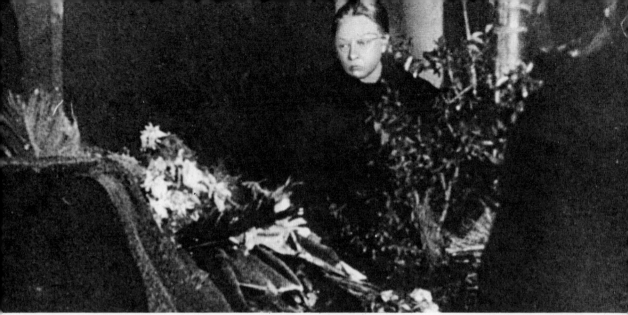

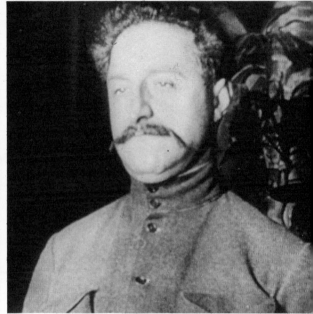

The body of Vladimir Ilich Lenin was transported to the Room of Columns in Moscow, where for four days his old Bolshevik companions and the people of Moscow kept vigil.

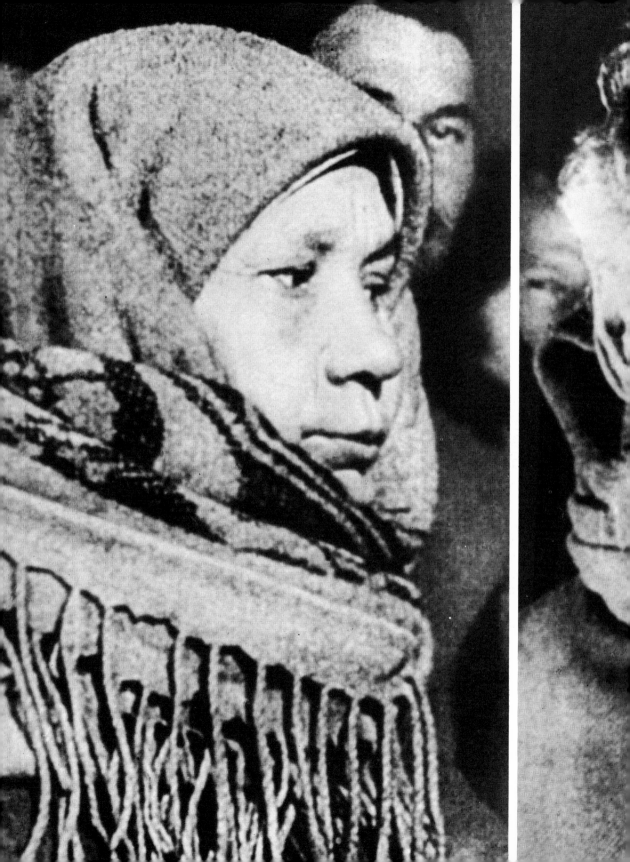

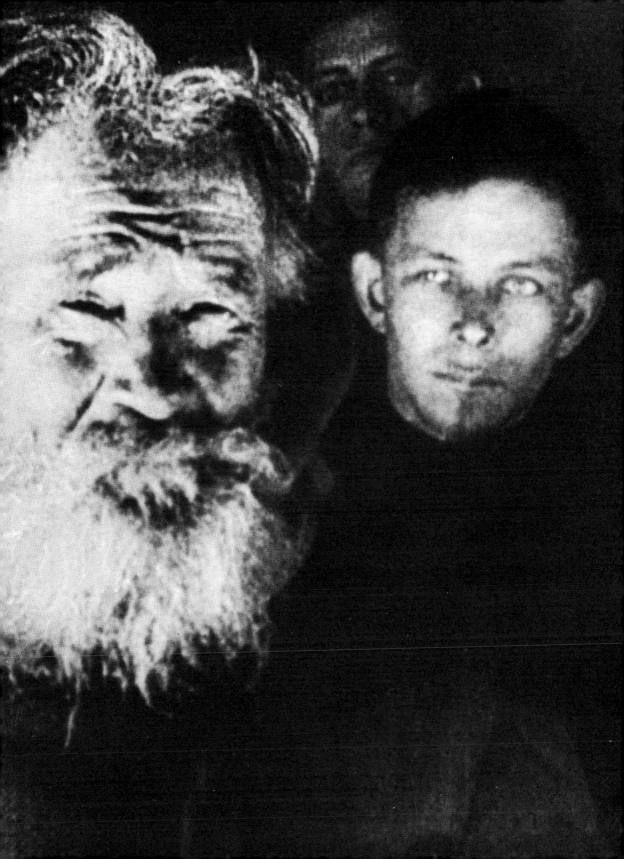

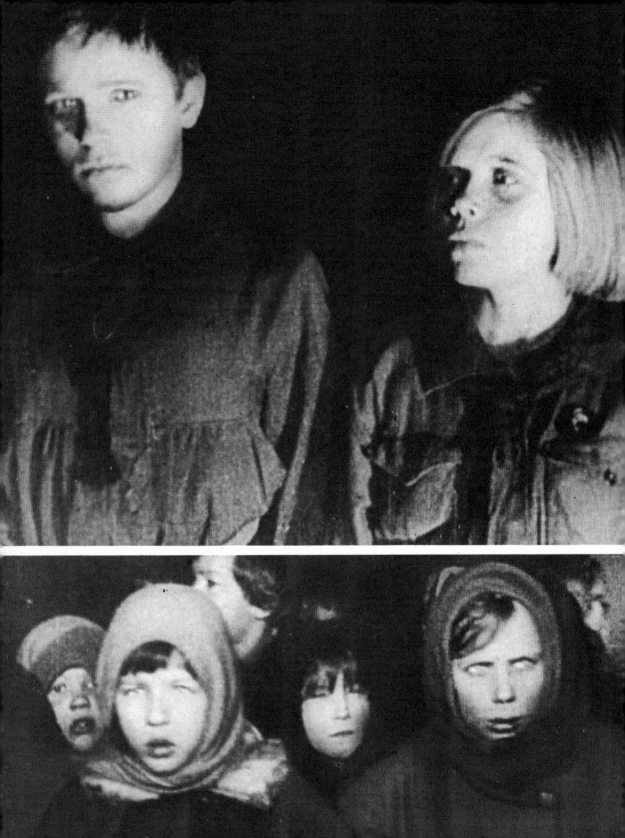

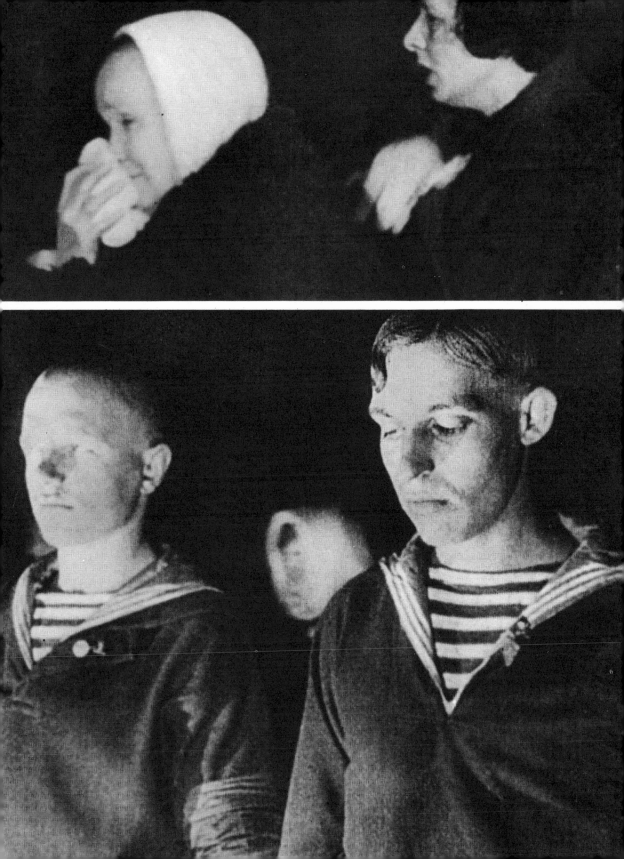

He had said: "The lives of our children will be better than ours. Much of what we have lived through will be spared them; their lives will be less cruel. But I do not envy them. Our generation accomplished a task of astounding historical importance. The cruelty of our lives, imposed by circumstances, will be understood and forgiven. Everything will be understood, everything!"

NOTE ON DATES: Dates in this book through January 31, 1918, are expressed according to the Julian calendar, then in use in Russia; those from February 1918 on, in the current Gregorian calendar. The shift advanced the date thirteen days; thus the anniversary of October 25, 1917, falls on November 7.

INDEX